# 24 Ways to Make Money Online with AI

## Navigate Financial Challenges with Sustainable Side Gigs

Allie A. Coke

**To My S&P**

Thanks for making sure I had enough of everything that really mattered.

**AAC**

# Table Of Contents

# Introduction

Welcome to the captivating world of Artificial Intelligence (AI) and its endless potential for earning money online. In our rapidly evolving digital landscape, where opportunities seem limitless, it is crucial to embrace the latest technologies. AI stands at the forefront of this revolution.

I introduce to you "24 Ways to Make Money Online with AI: Navigate Financial Challenges with Sustainable Side Gigs," a comprehensive guide resulting from my personal experiences with AI and my eagerness to explore even more possibilities in this incredible field. As an educator, I have always been fascinated by the concept of utilizing technology to promote learning, enhance skills, and create innovative avenues for generating income.

After years of teaching practical skills and then witnessing the transformative impact of AI, I became determined to share my knowledge and experiences with others. This book is not only thorough but also serves as a practical roadmap, providing 24 proven methods to make money online using AI.

Welcome to the future of online income generation!

# Navigate Financial Challenges with Sustainable Side Gigs

How can you navigate financial challenges with sustainable side gigs?

AI can play a vital role in helping you navigate financial challenges with sustainable side gigs by:

1. Assisting you in identifying suitable options for increasing income.
2. Providing opportunities for the development of your knowledge and skills.
3. Enabling access to gig marketplaces highlighted by the websites included in this book. (Please note that the list of websites is illustrative rather than exhaustive).
4. Facilitating financial management by optimizing income and minimizing risk.

# 1. Online Tutoring

## 1. Online Tutoring:

Teach subjects you excel in through platforms like Tutor.com or VIPKid.

### Requirements for Online Tutoring:

1. **Technical Setup:** A dependable computer or laptop, high-speed internet connection, webcam, microphone, and headphones are essential for smooth communication and interaction.
2. **Subject Proficiency:** A strong grasp of the subject you intend to tutor is vital for providing accurate and effective guidance to students.
3. **Communication Skills:** Clear and effective communication is crucial for explaining concepts, answering questions, and engaging students in an online setting.
4. **Teaching Resources:** Familiarity with online teaching tools, interactive whiteboards, screen-sharing applications, and relevant educational software enhances the quality of instruction.
5. **Time Management:** The ability to manage your schedule and dedicate consistent time to tutoring sessions is important for maintaining a structured learning experience.
6. **Adaptability:** Being adaptable to different learning styles and student needs ensures you can tailor your teaching methods accordingly.

Relevant Websites for Online Tutoring:

1. **Wyzant:** A platform connecting tutors with students seeking personalized instruction in various subjects.
2. **Chegg Tutors:** Offers on-demand tutoring in a wide range of subjects, allowing tutors to connect with students in real time.
3. **Tutor.com:** Provides access to expert tutors for instant assistance and guidance in various subjects.
4. **VIPKid:** Focuses on English language tutoring, connecting native English speakers with students in countries like China.
5. **Khan Academy:** Offers a wide array of educational resources and tools for tutors to provide supplementary instruction.

Advantages of Online Tutoring:

1. **Flexibility:** Online tutoring enables you to set your own schedule and reach students from different time zones, enhancing convenience for both tutors and learners.
2. **Global Reach:** You can connect with students from around the world, broadening your reach and exposure to diverse learning needs.
3. **Convenience:** Tutors and students can participate in sessions from the comfort of their homes, saving time and reducing commuting-related stress.
4. **Personalized Learning:** Online platforms often include features that allow tutors to customize lessons to match individual student learning styles and needs.
5. **Recorded Sessions:** Sessions can be recorded, allowing students to review the material at their own pace.

## Disadvantages of Online Tutoring:

1. **Technical Challenges:** Internet connectivity issues and technical glitches can disrupt the ow of sessions and hinder effective communication.
2. **Lack of Physical Interaction:** Online tutoring lacks the physical presence that can facilitate direct learning and certain teaching methods.
3. **Distractions:** Students might face distractions from their environment, affecting their focus and engagement during sessions.
4. **Communication Barriers:** Misinterpretation of cues and delayed responses due to online communication can lead to misunderstandings.
5. **Limited Non-verbal Communication:** Both tutors and students might miss non-verbal cues that play a role in traditional face-to-face teaching.

Online tutoring offers several benefits such as flexibility and global reach, but it also comes with challenges related to technology, communication, and the absence of physical presence. Tutors who can effectively navigate these challenges can create valuable learning experiences for their students.

## 2. Freelance Writing

## 2. Freelance Writing:

Offer your writing skills on platforms like Upwork or Freelancer.

### Requirements for Freelance Writing:

1. **Writing Skills:** A strong command of the English language, grammar, and writing style is essential for producing high-quality content.
2. **Creativity:** The ability to generate original and engaging ideas across diverse topics is crucial in freelance writing.
3. **Research Skills:** Freelance writers often need to research and gather information to create accurate and informative articles.
4. **Time Management:** Efficiently managing deadlines and juggling multiple projects is important for success in freelance writing.
5. **Communication:** Effective communication with clients, editors, and collaborators ensures that the content meets their requirements.
6. **Self-Motivation:** Freelance writers need to be self-driven and proactive in finding opportunities and improving their skills.

Relevant Websites for Freelance Writing:

1. **Upwork:** A platform where freelance writers can bid on a variety of writing projects, from articles to blog posts.
2. **Freelancer:** Offers a wide range of writing opportunities, including content creation, copywriting, and technical writing.
3. **Fiverr:** Freelance writers can create packages for different writing services and set their own prices.
4. **ProBlogger Job Board:** Specifically focuses on blogging and content creation jobs.
5. **Contently:** Connects freelance writers with brands and publications looking for content creation.

Advantages of Freelance Writing:

1. **Flexibility:** Freelance writers can set their own schedules and work from anywhere, providing an excellent work-life balance.
2. **Variety of Topics:** Writers have the opportunity to explore and write about a wide range of subjects, expanding their knowledge and expertise.
3. **Income Potential:** Freelance writing offers the potential to earn a substantial income, especially as writers gain experience and expertise.
4. **Skill Enhancement:** Writers continually improve their writing, research, and communication skills by working on diverse projects.
5. **Portfolio Building:** Freelancers can build a strong portfolio by working on different projects, which can attract more clients and higher-paying opportunities.

Disadvantages of Freelance Writing:

1. **Income Variability:** Income can be inconsistent, with periods of high demand and low demand affecting earnings.
2. **Uncertain Workload:** Freelancers might experience periods of heavy workload followed by quiet periods with less work available.
3. **Self-Employment Responsibilities:** Freelance writers are responsible for managing their taxes, invoicing, and other administrative tasks.
4. **Competition:** The freelance writing market can be competitive, making it important to continuously improve skills and stand out.
5. **Isolation:** Working independently can lead to feelings of isolation, especially if writers are not actively networking.

Freelance writing offers flexibility, the potential for a diverse range of topics, and the opportunity to earn a substantial income. However, it also comes with challenges like income variability and competition. Writers who can effectively manage these challenges can find success and fulfillment in the world of freelance writing.

# 3. Virtual Assistant

### 3. Virtual Assistant:

Provide administrative support remotely for busy professionals.

Requirements for Virtual Assistant:

1. **Organizational Skills:** Virtual assistants need to manage tasks, schedules, and information efficiently to support clients effectively.
2. **Communication Skills:** Clear and timely communication with clients and team members is essential for seamless collaboration.
3. **Tech Proficiency:** Familiarity with various software, tools, and communication platforms used for remote work is crucial.
4. **Multitasking:** Virtual assistants often manage multiple tasks simultaneously, so strong multitasking skills are important.
5. **Problem-Solving:** The ability to identify issues and find solutions independently is valuable in this role.
6. **Reliability:** Virtual assistants must be dependable and committed to meeting deadlines and fulfilling their responsibilities.

**Relevant Websites for Virtual Assistant Jobs:**

1. **Upwork:** Offers a wide range of virtual assistant opportunities in different industries and tasks.
2. **Freelancer:** Connects virtual assistants with clients seeking administrative and support services.
3. **Time Etc:** Specializes in providing virtual assistant services to entrepreneurs and businesses.
4. **Belay:** Offers virtual assistant positions primarily to support business owners and executives.
5. **Fiverr:** Allows virtual assistants to highlight their skills and offer numerous services to potential clients.

**Advantages of Being a Virtual Assistant:**

1. **Flexibility:** Virtual assistants can often set their own schedules and work from anywhere with an internet connection.
2. **Diverse Tasks:** VA roles involve a wide range of tasks, from administrative duties to social media management, offering variety in work.
3. **Remote Work:** This role eliminates the need for commuting and allows for a better work-life balance.
4. **Skill Development:** Virtual assistants can develop a versatile skill set through exposure to different tasks and industries.
5. **Global Clients:** Working virtually enables VAs to collaborate with clients from around the world, broadening their experience.

Disadvantages of Being a Virtual Assistant:

1. **Isolation:** Remote work might lead to feelings of isolation, as there is limited face-to-face interaction with colleagues.
2. **Variable Income:** Income might fluctuate based on the number of clients and projects available.
3. **Client Dependence:** Virtual assistants often rely on clients for consistent work, which can be unpredictable.
4. **Time Zone Challenges:** Collaborating with clients in different time zones can lead to communication and scheduling difficulties.
5. **Boundaries:** Establishing clear boundaries between work and personal life can be challenging when working from home.

Being a virtual assistant offers flexibility, a diverse workload, and the chance to develop a broad skill set. However, it comes with potential challenges like isolation and variable income. As the demand for remote work grows, virtual assistants play a vital role in supporting businesses and individuals in various capacities.

## 4. Social Media Management

### 4. Social Media Management:

Help businesses manage their social media presence and content.

Requirements for Social Media Management:

1. **Social Media Savviness:** A deep understanding of various social media platforms, trends, and best practices is crucial.
2. **Creativity:** The ability to craft engaging and visually appealing content that resonates with the target audience.
3. **Communication Skills:** Effective written communication for captions, posts, and responses is essential.
4. **Analytics Proficiency:** Understanding of social media analytics tools to track and analyze the performance of posts.
5. **Time Management:** Efficiently managing content scheduling, posting, and engagement across different platforms.
6. **Adaptability:** Being able to adjust strategies based on platform algorithm changes and audience preferences.

## Relevant Websites for Social Media Management Jobs:

1. **LinkedIn:** Job listings for various social media management positions can be found here.
2. **Indeed:** Offers a range of job opportunities for social media managers in different industries.
3. **Glassdoor:** Provides insights into company reviews and salaries for social media management roles.
4. **FlexJobs:** Focuses on remote and flexible job opportunities, including social media management.
5. **AngelList:** Particularly relevant for social media positions within startups and tech companies.

## Advantages of Social Media Management:

1. **Creativity:** Social media managers can express creativity through content creation and strategy development.
2. **Global Reach:** Social media enables businesses to reach a global audience and engage with diverse demographics.
3. **Brand Building:** Effective social media management helps build a strong brand identity and online presence.
4. **Real-Time Engagement:** Direct engagement with the audience allows for instant feedback and relationship-building.
5. **Measurable Results:** Analytics tools provide insights into post-performance, helping refine strategies.

**Disadvantages of Social Media Management:**

1. **Constant Monitoring:** Social media requires continuous monitoring and engagement, which can be time-consuming.
2. **Negative Feedback:** Managing negative comments and criticism can be challenging.
3. **Platform Changes:** Rapid changes in algorithms and features can impact content visibility and engagement.
4. **Pressure for Virality:** The pressure to create viral content can sometimes overshadow long-term brand-building efforts.
5. **Burnout:** The fast-paced nature of social media management can lead to burnout if not managed well.

Social media management offers opportunities for creativity, brand growth, and real-time interaction. However, it demands constant attention, adapting to changes, and effectively managing challenges such as negative feedback. Skilled social media managers play a pivotal role in shaping a brand's online presence and engagement with its audience.

# 5. Graphic Design

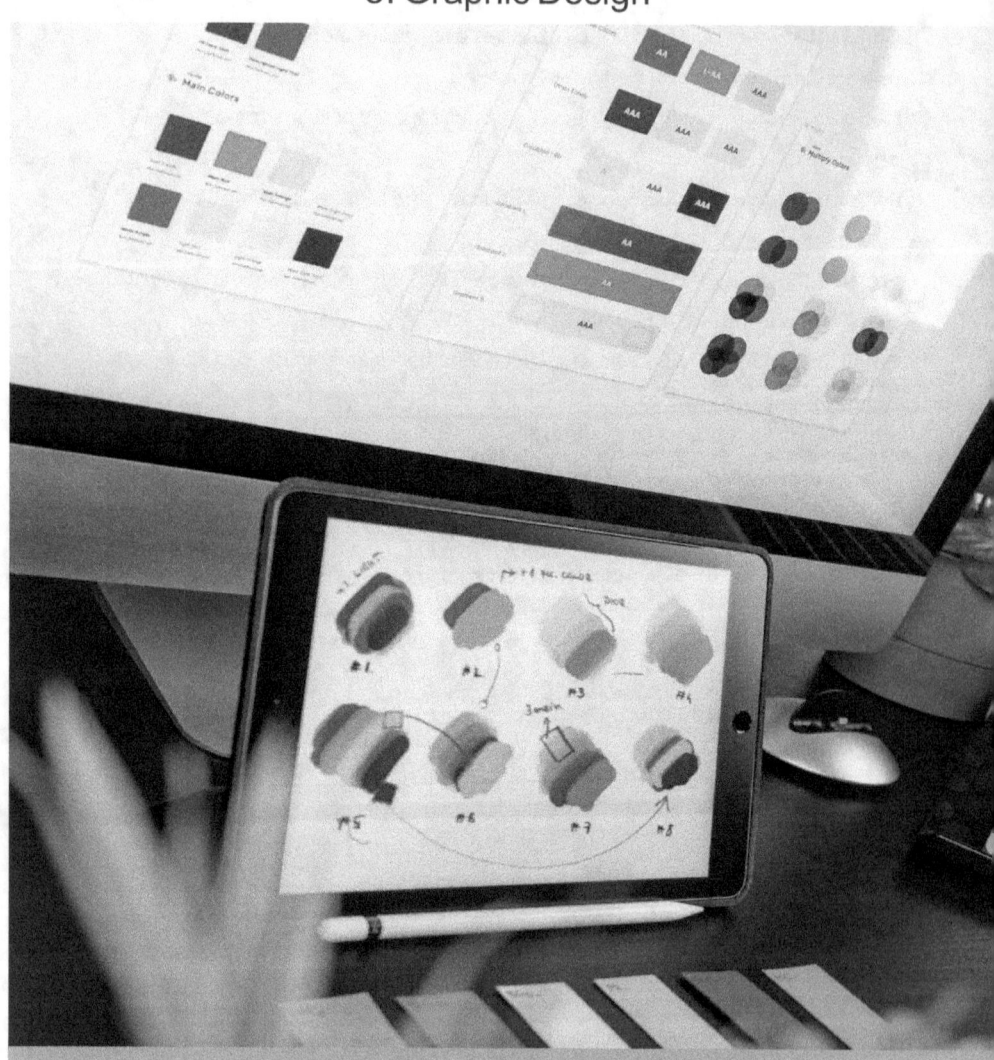

### 5. Graphic Design:

Create logos, banners, and other visual content for clients.

Requirements for Graphic Design:

1. **Design Skills:** Proficiency in design principles, typography, layout, and visual composition is essential.
2. **Software Proficiency:** Mastery of graphic design software like Adobe Creative Suite (Photoshop, Illustrator, InDesign) or other relevant tools.
3. **Creativity:** The ability to generate original and innovative design concepts for various projects.
4. **Attention to Detail:** Precise attention to details, color accuracy, and alignment in designs.
5. **Communication:** Effective communication to understand client needs and present design ideas.
6. **Portfolio:** Building a strong portfolio displaying a range of design work is important for attracting clients or employers.

**Relevant Websites for Graphic Design Jobs:**

1. **Behance:** A platform to highlight your portfolio and connect with potential clients and employers.
2. **Dribbble:** A community for designers to share their work and find freelance opportunities.
3. **Upwork:** Offers various graphic design projects where freelancers can bid on opportunities.
4. **Freelancer:** Connects graphic designers with clients seeking design services.
5. **99designs:** A platform for designers to participate in contests and projects for clients worldwide.
6. **Adobe Firefly**: A generative AI tool for the creation of image and text effects.

**Advantages of Graphic Design:**

1. **Creative Expression:** Graphic design allows designers to express their creativity through visual mediums.
2. **Diverse Projects:** Designers can work on a wide range of projects, from branding and marketing materials to web design and illustration.
3. **Freelance Opportunities:** Graphic designers often have the flexibility to work as freelancers, setting their own schedules.
4. **Impactful Communication:** Designers play a key role in visually communicating messages and ideas effectively.
5. **Portfolio Building:** Every project adds to a designer's portfolio, highlighting their skills and expertise.

**Disadvantages of Graphic Design:**

1. **Subjective Nature:** Design is subjective, and clients' preferences may differ from the designer's vision.
2. **Deadline Pressure:** Tight deadlines and multiple projects can lead to stress and burnout.
3. **Continuous Learning:** Staying updated with software updates and design trends requires ongoing learning.
4. **Client Communication Challenges:** Misunderstandings can arise if designers and clients do not effectively communicate expectations.
5. **Competition:** The field of graphic design is competitive, requiring designers to continuously stand out.

Graphic design offers opportunities for creativity, impact, and a diverse range of projects. However, designers need to navigate subjective preferences, manage deadlines, and keep up with industry changes. With the right skills and a strong portfolio, graphic designers can create visually compelling content that resonates with audiences.

# 6. Web Development

## 6. Web Development:

Build websites and web applications for individuals or businesses.

Requirements for Web Development:

1. **Programming Languages:** Proficiency in programming languages like HTML, CSS, JavaScript, and others depending on the scope of work.
2. **Front-End Development:** Knowledge of creating visually appealing and responsive user interfaces (UI) and user experiences (UX).
3. **Back-End Development:** Understanding of server-side scripting, databases, and server management for dynamic websites.
4. **Web Frameworks:** Familiarity with frameworks like React, Angular, or Vue for front-end development, and Django, Ruby on Rails, or Node.js for back-end.
5. **Version Control/Git:** Proficiency in the use of version control systems like Git for collaboration and code management.
6. **Problem-Solving:** Ability to troubleshoot issues and find solutions to technical challenges.

Relevant Websites for Web Development Jobs:

1. **LinkedIn:** Offers job listings for web development roles in various industries.
2. **Indeed:** Provides a range of web development opportunities, from entry-level to senior positions.
3. **Stack Overflow Jobs:** Focuses on tech-related jobs, including web development positions.
4. **GitHub Jobs:** Lists jobs related to software development, including web development.
5. **Freelance Platforms:** Websites like Upwork, Freelancer, and Toptal offer web development freelance opportunities.

Advantages of Web Development:

1. **High Demand:** Web developers are in constant demand as businesses and individuals need websites and applications.
2. **Creative Expression:** Web development allows for creative expression through designing and building digital interfaces.
3. **Remote Work:** Many web development roles offer remote work opportunities, providing flexibility.
4. **Continuous Learning:** The field evolves rapidly, providing ongoing opportunities for learning and skill enhancement.
5. **Variety of Projects:** Web developers can work on diverse projects, from e-commerce sites to web applications.

**Disadvantages of Web Development:**

1. **Rapid Changes:** The fast-paced nature of technology means developers must constantly adapt to new tools and frameworks.
2. **Technical Challenges:** Debugging and solving technical issues can be time-consuming and challenging.
3. **Client Communication:** Translating technical jargon into understandable terms for clients can be difficult.
4. **Long Hours:** Meeting deadlines or dealing with unexpected challenges might lead to long working hours.
5. **Continuous Learning:** While an advantage, the need for constant learning can also be a challenge for some.

Web development offers a dynamic career with a high demand for skilled professionals. However, it comes with the need for constant learning, technical challenges, and the responsibility of staying up to date with the latest trends. Skilled web developers play a crucial role in shaping the digital landscape.

# 7. Online Surveys

## 7. Online Surveys:

Participate in paid surveys on platforms like Survey Junkie or Swagbucks.

### Requirements for Online Surveys:

1. **Research Objective:** Clear understanding of the research goal and the information you aim to gather through the survey.
2. **Question Design:** Ability to create well-structured, unbiased, and relevant survey questions.
3. **Target Audience:** Define the specific demographic or group you want to target for your survey.
4. **Survey Platform:** Familiarity with online survey platforms that enable you to design, distribute, and analyze surveys.
5. **Data Analysis:** Basic data analysis skills to interpret survey responses and draw meaningful conclusions.
6. **Ethical Considerations:** Awareness of ethical guidelines when collecting and using survey data.

### Relevant Websites for Online Surveys:

1. **SurveyMonkey:** A popular platform for creating and distributing online surveys.
2. **Google Forms:** Offers a free and effortless way to create surveys using Google's tools.
3. **Qualtrics:** Provides advanced survey and research capabilities for businesses and researchers.
4. **Typeform:** Focuses on creating engaging and interactive surveys.
5. **Zoho Survey:** Offers tools to create surveys and analyze responses.

**Advantages of Online Surveys:**

1. **Ease of Distribution:** Online surveys can be distributed quickly through email, social media, or websites.
2. **Cost-Effective:** Conducting online surveys is more affordable than traditional methods.
3. **Wide Reach:** Surveys can reach a diverse and geographically dispersed audience.
4. **Faster Data Collection:** Online surveys allow for rapid data collection and analysis.
5. **Anonymity:** Respondents may feel more comfortable providing honest answers due to the anonymity of the survey.

**Disadvantages of Online Surveys:**

1. **Sampling Bias:** Online surveys might not represent the broader population accurately due to self-selection bias.
2. **Limited Depth:** Complex or in-depth questions might not be suitable for online surveys.
3. **Technical Challenges:** Respondents with limited internet access or technical skills might face difficulties.
4. **Low Response Rates:** Online surveys can have lower response rates compared to other methods.
5. **Data Quality:** Ensuring respondents provide accurate and thoughtful answers can be a challenge.

Online surveys offer a convenient and cost-effective way to gather data quickly. However, they can be limited by sampling bias and may not always provide in-depth insights. Effective survey design and a good understanding of the target audience are crucial to obtaining meaningful results.

## 8. Voiceover Work

## 8. Voiceover Work:

Offer your voice for commercials, audiobooks, or podcasts.

**Requirements for Voiceover Work:**

1. **Clear Pronunciation:** A clear and articulate speaking style is essential for effective communication.
2. **Versatility:** The ability to modulate your voice for different tones, emotions, and characters.
3. **Recording Equipment:** Access to high-quality recording equipment, including a microphone and soundproof space.
4. **Script Interpretation:** Skill in understanding and conveying the intended message and emotion from a script.
5. **Editing Skills:** Basic audio editing skills to clean up recordings and deliver professional-quality files.
6. **Language Skills:** Proficiency in the language(s) in which you will be providing voiceovers.

## Relevant Websites for Voiceover Work:

1. **Voices.com:** A platform connecting voice talent with clients seeking voiceovers for various projects.
2. **Voice123:** Offers opportunities for voice actors to audition for a wide range of voiceover projects.
3. **Fiverr:** Allows voiceover artists to create gigs and offer their services to potential clients.
4. **ACX (Audiobook Creation Exchange):** Connects voiceover artists with authors and publishers for audiobook projects.
5. **Upwork:** Offers opportunities for freelance voiceover work among other gigs.

## Advantages of Voiceover Work:

1. **Flexibility:** Voiceover work often allows for remote and flexible work arrangements.
2. **Creative Expression:** Voice artists can express creativity through diverse tones, accents, and characters.
3. **Global Reach:** Voiceovers can be used in projects that reach a global audience.
4. **Diverse Projects:** Voiceover work spans various industries, including commercials, animations, audiobooks, and more.
5. **Potential Income:** Skilled voiceover artists can earn a substantial income, especially for ongoing projects.

**Disadvantages of Voiceover Work:**

1. **Competition:** The field is competitive, with voiceover artists competing for similar projects.
2. **Audition Process:** Auditioning for roles can be time-consuming, and not all auditions lead to paid work.
3. **Variable Income:** Income can vary based on the number and type of projects available.
4. **Initial Investment:** Quality recording equipment and soundproofing setup might require an initial investment.
5. **Rejection:** Not all auditions lead to roles, and rejection can be a part of the process.

Voiceover work offers a chance to display creativity and talent while providing a flexible working environment. However, it comes with competition, auditioning challenges, and variable income. Skilled voiceover artists who can effectively market themselves and adapt to client needs can find success in this field.

## 9. Stock Photography

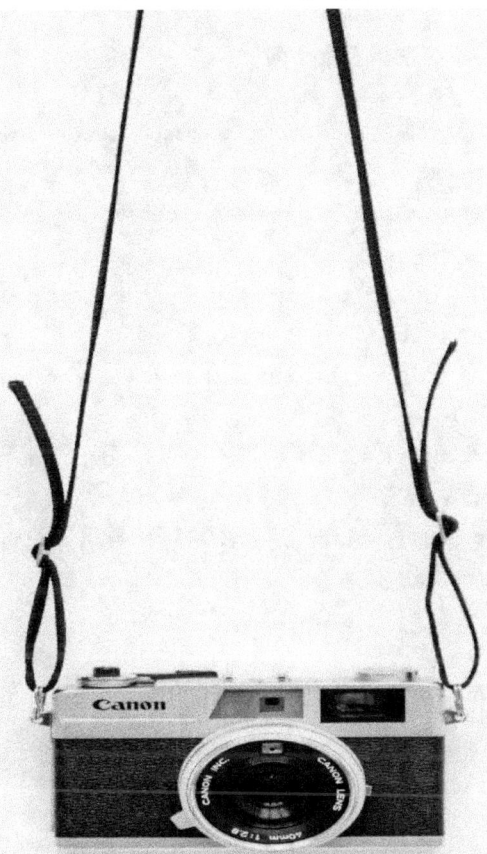

## 9. Stock Photography:

**Sell your photos on platforms like Shutterstock or Adobe Stock.**

**Requirements for Stock Photography:**

1. **Photography Skills:** Proficiency in photography techniques, including composition, lighting, and framing.
2. **Quality Equipment:** Access to a high-resolution camera and lenses that produce clear and sharp images.
3. **Image Editing:** Skill in post-processing and editing to enhance and re ne photographs.
4. **Conceptualization:** Ability to create images that convey concepts, emotions, and stories.
5. **Legal Knowledge:** Understanding of copyright laws and licensing agreements for stock photography.
6. **Submission Guidelines:** Familiarity with the requirements and guidelines of stock photography platforms.

## Relevant Websites for Stock Photography:

1. **Shutterstock:** A popular platform for photographers to sell their images to a global market.
2. **Getty Images:** Offers opportunities for photographers to license their work for various purposes.
3. **Adobe Stock:** Allows photographers to sell their images directly through Adobe's creative ecosystem.
4. **iStock:** A subsidiary of Getty Images, offering another platform for photographers to sell their images.
5. **Unsplash:** A platform for sharing high-quality, free-to-use images, with the option to receive donations.

## Advantages of Stock Photography:

1. **Passive Income:** Once uploaded, stock photos can generate income over time with each sale.
2. **Global Reach:** Clients can purchase stock photos worldwide for various purposes.
3. **Diverse Uses:** Images can be used in advertising, websites, publications, presentations, and more.
4. **Creative Expression:** Photographers can demonstrate their artistic skills through a variety of subjects and styles.
5. **Portfolio Building:** Stock photography contributes to building a diverse portfolio.

Disadvantages of Stock Photography:

1. **Competition:** The stock photography market is saturated, making it challenging to stand out.
2. **Royalty Rates:** Some platforms offer low royalty rates, impacting potential earnings.
3. **Licensing Restrictions:** Photographers must adhere to specific licensing terms and usage restrictions.
4. **Rejection:** Not all submitted images are accepted by stock platforms, leading to potential disappointment.
5. **Time Investment:** Uploading, keywording, and managing images can be time-consuming.

Stock photography offers the potential for passive income and exposure but is accompanied by fierce competition and varying royalty rates. Photographers who understand market trends, create high-quality images, and effectively manage their portfolio can find success in the stock photography industry.

# 10. Language Translation

## 10. Language Translation:
### Translate written content from one language to another.

**Requirements for Language Translation:**

1. **Bilingual Proficiency:** Fluency in at least two languages, including strong writing skills in both languages.
2. **Cultural Understanding:** Deep understanding of cultural nuances and context to accurately convey meaning.
3. **Grammar and Syntax:** A good understanding of grammar is required in addition to an appreciation of idiomatic expressions in both languages.
4. **Research Skills:** Ability to research terminology and concepts specific to various subjects.
5. **Mindfulness:** Keen attention to detail to ensure accuracy and fidelity to the original content.
6. **Translation Tools:** Familiarity with translation software and tools to enhance productivity.

**Relevant Websites for Language Translation Jobs:**

1. **ProZ:** A platform connecting freelance translators with clients seeking language translation services.
2. **TranslatorsCafe:** Offers a job board and networking opportunities for translators.
3. **Upwork:** Freelancers can find translation projects among other opportunities.
4. **Gengo:** Offers opportunities for freelance translation work on a wide range of topics.
5. **One Hour Translation:** Provides a platform for freelance translators to work on various projects.

Advantages of Language Translation:

1. **Global Opportunities:** Translators can work on projects that connect diverse cultures and languages.
2. **Remote Work:** Many translation roles offer remote work options, allowing for flexible arrangements.
3. **Skill Enhancement:** Translators continuously improve their language skills and learn about various subjects.
4. **Diverse Projects:** Translation work spans industries like business, literature, legal, medical, and more.
5. **Cultural Exchange:** Translators engage with diverse content, gaining insights into various cultures.

Disadvantages of Language Translation:

1. **Subjective Nature:** Different interpretations can lead to variations in translated content.
2. **Deadlines:** Meeting tight deadlines for translation projects can be demanding.
3. **Language Evolution:** Languages evolve, requiring translators to stay updated on language changes.
4. **Emotional Toll:** Translating sensitive or emotional content can take an emotional toll.
5. **Competition:** The field is competitive, with many translators offering similar services.

Language translation offers a gateway to global communication and cultural exchange. However, it comes with challenges related to accuracy, deadlines, and the subjective nature of translation. Skillful translators who understand the intricacies of language and culture play a crucial role in bridging communication gaps.

## 11. Online Coaching

### 11. Online Coaching:

Provide guidance and support to clients in areas like fitness or personal development.

**Requirements for Online Coaching:**

1. **Expertise:** In-depth knowledge and expertise in the subject or skill you intend to coach. Popular coaching topics include fitness, effective communication, leadership, career development, personal development, work-life balance, and stress management.
2. **Communication Skills:** Effective communication skills are required to convey information clearly and effectively.
3. **People Skills:** The ability to build rapport and establish a strong coach-client relationship.
4. **Technology Proficiency:** Familiarity with online communication tools for virtual coaching sessions.
5. **Goal Setting:** Skill in setting achievable goals and designing personalized coaching plans.
6. **Empathy:** The capacity to understand and empathize with clients' needs and challenges.

**Relevant Websites for Online Coaching:**

1. **Coach.me:** Connects coaches with clients seeking guidance in various areas, from fitness to career.
2. **BetterHelp:** Focuses on online counseling and therapy services for mental health professionals.
3. **GrowthMentor:** A platform connecting mentors and experts with individuals seeking guidance.
4. **The Muse:** Offers career coaching services for professionals seeking career advancement.
5. **Udemy:** Allows coaches to create and sell online courses in their areas of expertise.

**Advantages of Online Coaching:**

1. **Global Reach:** Online coaching allows you to collaborate with clients from around the world.
2. **Flexibility:** Coaches can set their own schedules and work from any location.
3. **Convenience:** Both coaches and clients can participate in sessions from the comfort of their homes.
4. **Diverse Topics:** Online coaching covers a wide range of subjects, from personal development to business.
5. **Personalization:** Coaching plans can be tailored to individual client needs and goals.

Disadvantages of Online Coaching:

1. **Technical Challenges:** Internet connectivity issues and technology glitches can disrupt sessions.
2. **Lack of In-Person Interaction:** Online coaching lacks the physical presence that some clients prefer.
3. **Miscommunication:** Online communication might lead to misunderstandings or misinterpretations.
4. **Accountability:** Some clients might struggle with self-discipline and accountability in a virtual setting.
5. **Privacy Concerns:** Clients might have concerns about the privacy and security of online interactions.

Online coaching offers a convenient and flexible way to provide guidance and support to clients. However, it comes with challenges like technical issues and potential miscommunication. Skilled online coaches who can build strong relationships and deliver valuable insights can create impactful coaching experiences for their clients.

# 12. Virtual Event Planning

### 12. Virtual Event Planning:

Help individuals or organizations plan and execute online events.

**Requirements for Virtual Event Planning:**

1. **Event Management Skills:** Proficiency in planning, organizing, and executing events.
2. **Technology Proficiency:** Familiarity with virtual event platforms, streaming tools, and communication software.
3. **Creativity:** Ability to design engaging and interactive virtual experiences for participants.
4. **Logistical Planning:** Skill in coordinating schedules, speakers, sessions, and technical aspects.
5. **Communication:** Effective communication skills to consult with clients, speakers, sponsors, and attendees.
6. **Problem-Solving:** Capability to troubleshoot technical issues and adapt to unforeseen challenges.

**Relevant Websites for Virtual Event Planning:**

1. **Hopin:** A popular platform for hosting virtual events, offering various features like networking and sessions.
2. **Eventbrite:** Known for in-person events, it also supports virtual event hosting and promotion.
3. **Cvent:** Offers comprehensive event management solutions, including virtual event features.
4. **Zoom Events:** Integrates with Zoom to provide tools for hosting virtual conferences, webinars, and more.
5. **Bizzabo:** Focuses on end-to-end event management, including virtual events and hybrid options.

**Advantages of Virtual Event Planning:**

1. **Global Reach:** Virtual events can connect participants from around the world, expanding the audience.
2. **Cost Savings:** Virtual events can be more cost-effective than traditional in-person events.
3. **Flexibility:** Virtual events offer flexibility in terms of location and scheduling.
4. **Data Insights:** Online platforms provide data on attendee engagement and interactions.
5. **Environmentally Friendly:** Virtual events reduce the carbon footprint associated with travel and physical venues.

**Disadvantages of Virtual Event Planning:**

1. **Technical Challenges:** Technical issues like connectivity problems can impact the participant experience.
2. **Lack of Networking:** Virtual events might lack the in-person networking opportunities of physical events.
3. **Engagement:** Keeping participants engaged and focused in a virtual setting can be challenging.
4. **Learning Curve:** Attendees and organizers might need time to adapt to new virtual platforms.
5. **Dependence on Technology:** Technical failures can disrupt the event and cause frustration.

Virtual event planning offers a dynamic and versatile way to connect audiences, but it requires careful planning, technical proficiency, and creative solutions to engage participants effectively. Successful virtual event planners can create memorable and impactful experiences that transcend physical boundaries.

# 13. E-Commerce

### 14. E-Commerce:

Start an online store selling products in stock or dropshipping products without inventory from a third-party supplier directly to customers.

Requirements for E-commerce:

1. **Product or Service:** A viable product or service to sell to a target market.
2. **E-commerce Platform:** Access to a user-friendly and secure e-commerce platform.
3. **Product Information:** Detailed and accurate product descriptions, images, and pricing.
4. **Payment Gateway:** Integration with a reliable payment gateway to process transactions.
5. **Shipping and Logistics:** A system to manage shipping, tracking, and delivery to customers.
6. **Customer Support:** Responsive customer support to address inquiries and resolve issues.

Relevant Websites for E-commerce:

1. **Shopify:** A popular e-commerce platform for creating online stores and selling products.
2. **WooCommerce:** An e-commerce plugin for WordPress websites, suitable for various businesses.
3. **Amazon:** A leading online marketplace for selling products to a global audience.
4. **eBay:** Offers a platform for auction-style and fixed-price selling of various products.
5. **Etsy:** Focuses on handmade, vintage, and unique items, attracting a niche audience.

Advantages of E-commerce:

1. **Global Reach:** E-commerce allows businesses to reach customers worldwide.
2. **Convenience:** Customers can shop 24/7 from the comfort of their homes.
3. **Cost Efficiency:** Running an online store can have lower overhead costs compared to physical stores.
4. **Data Insights:** E-commerce platforms provide valuable data on customer behavior and preferences.
5. **Scalability:** E-commerce businesses can scale quickly without the need for physical expansion.

Disadvantages of E-commerce:

1. **Competition:** The online marketplace is highly competitive, requiring unique selling points.
2. **Technical Challenges:** Managing and maintaining an e-commerce website requires technical expertise.
3. **Customer Trust:** Gaining customer trust and ensuring secure transactions is crucial.
4. **Shipping Complexity:** Managing shipping coordination and costs can be challenging.
5. **Lack of Tangibility:** Customers cannot physically touch or try products before purchasing.

E-commerce offers businesses a global marketplace with convenience and cost-efficiency. However, it comes with challenges such as competition, technical requirements, and the need to build customer trust. Successful e-commerce ventures require effective marketing strategies, strong customer service, and a user-friendly online shopping experience.

## 14. Podcast Editing

### 14. Podcast Editing:

Edit and produce podcasts for individuals or businesses.

**Requirements for Podcast Editing:**

1. **Audio Editing Software:** Proficiency in using audio editing software like Audacity, Adobe Audition, or Reaper.
2. **Sound Quality:** Understanding of audio quality, noise reduction, and audio enhancement techniques.
3. **Editing Skills:** Ability to edit out mistakes, pauses, ums, ahs, and background noises.
4. **Content Flow:** Skill in maintaining a smooth and engaging flow of the podcast episode.
5. **Intro/Outro:** Adding music, intros, outros, and sound effects to enhance the podcast.
6. **Communication:** Effective communication with podcast hosts to understand their editing preferences.

**Relevant Websites for Podcast Editing:**

1. **Upwork:** Connects podcasters with freelance editors for podcast editing projects.
2. **Fiverr:** Offers a platform for podcasters to find editors for various podcast-related tasks.
3. **PodcastEditing.com:** A platform that specializes in offering podcast editing services.
4. **Freelance Platforms:** Websites like Freelancer and Guru have listings for podcast editing services.
5. **Networking:** Building a network within the podcasting community can lead to editing opportunities.

**Advantages of Podcast Editing:**

1. **Quality Enhancement:** Editing improves audio quality, removes distractions, and ensures professional content.
2. **Engagement:** Well-edited podcasts keep listeners engaged and enhance the overall listening experience.
3. **Time Savings:** Outsourcing editing frees up podcast hosts' time for content creation and other tasks.
4. **Consistency:** Editing helps maintain a consistent style and tone across podcast episodes.
5. **Brand Identity:** Custom intros, outros, and sound effects contribute to building a recognizable brand.

Disadvantages of Podcast Editing:

1. **Time-Consuming:** Editing podcasts can be time-consuming, especially for longer episodes.
2. **Technical Expertise:** Effective editing requires a good understanding of audio editing software.
3. **Dependency:** Relying on editors can lead to delays if edits are not completed on time.
4. **Cost:** Hiring professional editors can incur additional costs for podcast production.
5. **Communication Challenges:** Misunderstandings in editing preferences can lead to rework.

Podcast editing ensures high-quality content and engagement but requires technical skills and investment. Outsourcing editing can save time but also introduces a dependency on editors. Skilled podcast editors play a crucial role in enhancing the overall podcast experience for listeners.

# 15. App Development

### 15. App Development:

Create and sell a mobile phone app for your own courses.

Requirements for App Development:

1. **Course Content:** Well-structured and engaging course content to be included in the app.
2. **App Development Skills:** Proficiency in mobile app development, including programming languages like Java or Swift.
3. **User Interface (UI) Design:** Skill in designing an intuitive and user-friendly interface for the app.
4. **Content Management System (CMS):** Integration of a CMS to manage and update course content.
5. **Multimedia Integration:** Incorporation of multimedia elements such as videos, quizzes, and interactive features.
6. **Mobile Platform Knowledge:** Understanding of the specific requirements and guidelines for app stores (Google Play Store, Apple App Store).

Relevant Websites for App Development:

1. **Apple Developer:** Provides resources and tools for developing and publishing apps on the Apple App Store.
2. **Android Developers:** Offers guidance for building and distributing apps on the Google Play Store.
3. **Udemy:** Provides courses on app development for various platforms.
4. **Coursera:** Offers courses on mobile app development and related skills.
5. **GitHub:** Offers repositories and resources for app developers to collaborate and learn.

**Advantages of Creating and Selling a Course App:**

1. **Direct Reach:** An app allows direct access to course content for learners.
2. **Interactive Learning:** Apps can incorporate interactive elements, enhancing engagement.
3. **Branding:** An app can establish your brand and credibility as an educator.
4. **Monetization:** Selling courses through the app can provide a source of income.
5. **Convenience:** Learners can access course materials on-the-go using their mobile devices.

**Disadvantages of Creating and Selling a Course App:**

1. **Development Complexity:** App development requires technical skills and resources.
2. **Maintenance:** Regular updates and bug fixes are necessary to ensure the app's functionality.
3. **Competition:** The app marketplace is competitive, requiring a unique value proposition.
4. **Marketing:** Promoting the app and attracting users may be challenging.
5. **Platform Restrictions:** Adhering to guidelines of different app stores can be limiting.

Creating and selling a course app offers direct engagement and monetization opportunities. However, it requires technical expertise, ongoing maintenance, and effective marketing strategies. Success in this endeavor depends on providing valuable content, delivering a great user experience, and effectively promoting the app to your target audience.

## 16. Developing and Selling Online Courses

### 16. Developing and Selling Online Courses:

Create and deliver online courses for platforms such as Udemy or Teachable

Requirements for Developing Online Courses:

1. **Expertise:** In-depth knowledge and expertise in the subject matter of the course.
2. **Course Content:** Well-structured and engaging course content, including videos, quizzes, and resources.
3. **Presentation Skills:** Ability to convey information clearly and engagingly through video lectures.
4. **Video Production:** Basic video production skills to create high-quality video content.
5. **Platform Familiarity:** Familiarity with the chosen course platform's tools and features.
6. **Marketing Knowledge:** Understanding of online marketing to promote the course effectively.

**Relevant Websites for Selling Online Courses:**

1. **Udemy:** A popular platform for instructors to create and sell courses to a global audience.
2. **Teachable:** Allows instructors to create and customize their own online course websites.
3. **Skillshare:** Focuses on creative and practical classes, offering a subscription-based model.
4. **Coursera:** Partners with universities and institutions to offer a wide range of online courses.
5. **Thinkific:** Offers tools to create, market, and sell online courses.
6. **Passion.io:** Provides templates that can be used to create content to share skills via mobile apps on iOS, Google, and the web. It can be used to generate recurring revenue through online course participation and client engagement. Monthly subscription includes online support throughout the process.

**Advantages of Developing and Selling Online Courses:**

1. **Global Reach:** Online courses can reach a worldwide audience, expanding your reach.
2. **Passive Income:** Once created, courses can generate income over time with each enrollment.
3. **Flexibility:** You can create courses on your schedule and update content as needed.
4. **Skill Sharing:** Sharing your expertise allows you to impact and help others in your field.
5. **Branding:** Developing courses can establish your brand as an expert in your industry.

Disadvantages of Developing and Selling Online Courses:

1. **Initial Effort:** Creating high-quality course content requires considerable time and effort.
2. **Competition:** Online course platforms are saturated with courses on diverse topics.
3. **Marketing Challenge:** Effective promotion is necessary to stand out among other courses.
4. **Course Maintenance:** Regular updates and responding to student questions require ongoing attention.
5. **Income Variability:** Earnings can vary based on course popularity and enrollments.

Developing and selling online courses can be a fulfilling endeavor, allowing you to share your expertise and generate income. However, it requires commitment, effective marketing strategies, and continuous efforts to maintain course quality and engagement. A well-crafted course that addresses learner needs and provides value can lead to a successful online teaching venture.

# 17. Website Testing

### 17. Website Testing:

Test websites and provide feedback on user experience.

Requirements for Website Testing:

1. **Attention to Detail:** Keen attention to detail to identify issues and inconsistencies in the website.
2. **Technical Skills:** Basic understanding of web technologies, browsers, and devices.
3. **Problem-Solving:** Ability to identify and solve issues.
4. **Communication Skills:** Effective communication to report bugs and provide clear feedback.
5. **Test Environment:** Access to different browsers, devices, and operating systems for comprehensive testing.
6. **User Experience:** Understanding of user expectations and interactions on websites.

Relevant Websites for Website Testing:

1. **UserTesting:** Offers opportunities to evaluate websites and provide user feedback.
2. **Testbirds:** Provides crowdtesting services for website and app testing.
3. **TryMyUI:** Allows users to assess websites and apps and provide usability feedback.
4. **Enroll:** Offers usability testing for websites, apps, and products.
5. **UsabilityHub:** Provides user testing and feedback services for websites.

**Advantages of Website Testing:**

1. **Quality Assurance:** Testing ensures that websites function correctly and provide a positive user experience.
2. **Bug Identification:** Testing helps identify and fix bugs before they impact users.
3. **Usability Enhancement:** User feedback contributes to improving website usability and navigation.
4. **Enhanced Performance:** Testing helps optimize website performance and load times.
5. **Client Satisfaction:** Thorough testing leads to higher client satisfaction and user engagement.

**Disadvantages of Website Testing:**

1. **Time-Consuming:** Comprehensive testing requires time and effort, especially for larger websites.
2. **Resource Intensive:** Testing across different devices and browsers can be resource intensive.
3. **Subjective Feedback:** User feedback can be subjective and vary based on individual preferences.
4. **Scope Limitation:** Not all issues might be identified during testing, leading to potential surprises.
5. **Technical Challenges:** Deeper technical issues might require expertise to diagnose and fix.

Website testing is crucial for ensuring a smooth user experience and identifying potential issues before they affect users. It offers quality assurance and user-centric improvements but can be time-consuming and resource-intensive. Effective testing contributes to building user trust and satisfaction in websites.

# 18. Online Travel Agent

## 18. Online Travel Agent:

Help individuals plan and book their travel arrangements.

### Requirements for Becoming an Online Travel Agent:

1. **Travel Knowledge:** In-depth knowledge of travel destinations, accommodations, transportation, and attractions.
2. **Customer Service Skills:** Excellent customer service and communication skills to assist travelers.
3. **Booking Platforms:** Familiarity with online booking platforms for flights, hotels, cruises, and tours.
4. **Negotiation Skills:** Ability to secure deals and discounts for clients through effective negotiation.
5. **Organizational Skills:** Strong organizational skills to manage multiple bookings and itineraries.
6. **Legal Knowledge:** Understanding of travel regulations, visas, and insurance requirements.

### Relevant Websites for Online Travel Agents:

1. **Expedia:** Offers a platform for booking flights, hotels, and vacation packages.
2. **Booking.com:** Provides a wide range of accommodations and travel services.
3. **Priceline:** Offers deals on flights, hotels, and rental cars.
4. **Travelocity:** Allows users to book flights, hotels, and vacation packages.
5. **TripAdvisor:** Offers reviews, recommendations, and booking options for travel services.

**Advantages of Being an Online Travel Agent:**

1. **Flexibility:** Online travel agents can work remotely and manage their schedules.
2. **Commissions:** Earnings come from commissions on bookings, potentially leading to income growth.
3. **Travel Perks:** Agents may receive discounts or complimentary stays for personal travel.
4. **Variety:** Helping clients plan diverse trips provides a dynamic and engaging work environment.
5. **Client Relationships:** Building rapport with clients can lead to repeat business and referrals.

**Disadvantages of Being an Online Travel Agent:**

1. **Competition:** The online travel industry is competitive, requiring differentiation.
2. **Seasonal Demand:** Travel bookings might vary based on seasons and external factors.
3. **Customer Expectations:** Meeting diverse client expectations and preferences can be challenging.
4. **Dependence on Platforms:** Online travel agents rely on booking platforms for commissions.
5. **Uncertain Income:** Income can fluctuate depending on booking volume and client needs.

Becoming an online travel agent offers flexibility, the potential for earning commissions, and the opportunity to help clients create memorable travel experiences. However, it requires continuous adaptation to industry changes, effective customer service, and staying updated on travel trends. Skilled agents who provide personalized service and value can thrive in the competitive online travel industry.

# 19. Online Focus Groups

### 19. Online Focus Groups:

Participate in market research studies and provide feedback.

Requirements for Participating in Online Focus Groups:

1. **Internet Connection:** Access to a stable internet connection for participating in virtual discussions.
2. **Microphone and Webcam:** A microphone and webcam for effective communication and engagement.
3. **Opinions and Feedback:** Willingness to share honest opinions and provide valuable feedback.
4. **Communication Skills:** Ability to express thoughts clearly and contribute to group discussions.
5. **Availability:** Availability during scheduled focus group sessions.
6. **Demographic Fit:** Some focus groups might require specific demographics for research purposes.

Relevant Websites for Finding Online Focus Groups:

1. **Vindale Research:** Offers opportunities to participate in online surveys and focus groups.
2. **User Interviews:** Connects participants with companies seeking feedback through online interviews.
3. **Respondent:** Matches participants with relevant online research studies and focus groups.
4. **Survey Junkie:** Provides opportunities to participate in surveys and occasional focus groups.
5. **Engage In Depth:** Offers online market research studies and focus group participation.

Advantages of Participating in Online Focus Groups:

1. **Convenience:** Online focus groups can be participated in from the comfort of your own space.
2. **Flexible Schedule:** Many online groups offer a range of time options for sessions.
3. **Diverse Topics:** Participants can contribute to discussions on a wide range of subjects.
4. **Compensation:** Participants often receive compensation or rewards for their input.
5. **Global Reach:** Online focus groups can include participants from various locations.

Disadvantages of Participating in Online Focus Groups:

1. **Technical Issues:** Connectivity or technical problems can disrupt discussions.
2. **Limited Interaction:** Online interactions might not replicate the depth of face-to-face discussions.
3. **Group Dynamics:** Online dynamics can vary, affecting the quality of discussions.
4. **Privacy Concerns:** Sharing private opinions and data online can raise privacy concerns.
5. **Subjective Data:** The quality of insights can vary based on participant contributions.

Participating in online focus groups offers flexibility and compensation for sharing opinions and feedback. However, it comes with challenges related to technical issues and potential limitations in replicating the depth of in-person discussions. Effective participation and open communication can contribute to valuable insights for market research and other purposes.

## 20. AI Customer Support

### 20. AI Customer Support:

Work with organizations to develop and manage AI-powered customer support solutions.

**Requirements for AI Customer Support:**

1. **AI Technology Knowledge:** Proficiency in understanding and implementing AI-powered customer support systems.
2. **Data Analysis:** Skill in analyzing customer data to improve AI interactions.
3. **Communication Skills:** Ability to design AI responses that are clear and customer friendly.
4. **Problem-Solving:** Developing AI solutions that effectively address customer queries and issues.
5. **Integration:** Familiarity with integrating AI systems with existing customer support platforms.
6. **Monitoring and Improvement:** Constantly monitoring AI performance and optimizing responses.

**Relevant Websites for AI Customer Support Solutions:**

1. **Zendesk:** Offers AI-powered customer support solutions and integrations.
2. **Freshdesk:** Provides AI-driven features to enhance customer support interactions.
3. **IBM Watson:** Offers AI chatbot and virtual assistant solutions for customer support.
4. **Chatfuel:** Allows businesses to build AI-powered chatbots for customer interactions.
5. **Intercom:** Offers AI-based solutions for managing customer communication and support.

**Advantages of AI Customer Support:**

1. **24/7 Availability:** AI can provide round-the-clock support, improving customer service availability.
2. **Efficiency:** AI can manage a high volume of inquiries simultaneously, reducing wait times.
3. **Consistency:** AI responses are consistent and unaffected by mood or fatigue.
4. **Cost Savings:** AI support reduces the need for hiring and training additional human agents.
5. **Data Utilization:** AI gathers data on customer interactions, helping in identifying trends and improving services.

**Disadvantages of AI Customer Support:**

1. **Lack of Empathy:** AI might lack the emotional intelligence and empathy of human agents.
2. **Complex Issues:** AI may struggle with complex issues that require nuanced understanding.
3. **Technical Errors:** Glitches and technical issues can lead to incorrect or frustrating responses.
4. **Initial Setup:** Implementing AI systems requires initial investment and integration.
5. **Customer Frustration:** Inaccurate responses can frustrate customers and damage relationships.

AI customer support offers efficiency and accessibility but comes with challenges related to empathy and managing complex issues. The successful implementation of AI systems requires careful planning, continuous monitoring, and a balance between automation and human interaction. When used effectively, AI can enhance customer service and streamline support processes.

# 21. Online Resume Writing

### 21. Online Resume Writing:

Help individuals create professional resumes and cover letters.

**Requirements for Online Resume Writing:**

1. **Writing Skills:** Strong writing skills to create compelling and error-free resumes.
2. **Understanding of Industry:** Knowledge of various industries and job roles to tailor resumes accordingly.
3. **Communication Skills:** Ability to communicate effectively with clients to understand their background and goals.
4. **Formatting Expertise:** Proficiency in using formatting tools to create visually appealing resumes.
5. **Research Skills:** Skill in researching specific job requirements and incorporating relevant keywords.
6. **Attention to Detail:** Keen attention to detail to accurately represent clients' qualifications.

**Relevant Websites for Online Resume Writing:**

1. **TopResume:** Offers professional resume writing services for various industries.
2. **ResumeWriterDirect:** Provides personalized resume writing services for clients.
3. **CraftResumes:** Offers resume writing and design services for job seekers.
4. **ResumeGo:** Specializes in creating ATS-friendly resumes that get noticed by employers.
5. **Fiverr:** Provides a platform for freelance resume writers offering a range of services.

**Advantages of Online Resume Writing:**

1. **Professionalism:** Expert writers can create resumes that highlight clients' strengths effectively.
2. **Time Savings:** Hiring a professional saves time compared to crafting a resume from scratch.
3. **Tailored Content:** Writers can tailor resumes for specific job roles and industries.
4. **Keyword Optimization:** Resumes can be optimized with keywords to pass through Applicant Tracking Systems (ATS).
5. **Impactful Presentation:** Professional formatting and design can make resumes stand out.

**Disadvantages of Online Resume Writing:**

1. **Cost:** Professional resume writing services can incur a cost, especially for personalized assistance.
2. **Lack of Personal Touch:** Remote services might lack the in-person consultation experience.
3. **Dependency:** Relying solely on professional writers might hinder personal growth in resume writing skills.
4. **Varied Quality:** Quality of online resume writing services can vary widely.
5. **Privacy Concerns:** Sharing personal information online raises privacy and security concerns.

Online resume writing services offer expertise and efficiency in crafting effective resumes, but they come with costs and potential variations in quality. Job seekers should weigh the advantages against the potential disadvantages to determine the best approach for their individual needs.

## 22. Video Editing

## 22. Video Editing:

### Edit and produce videos for individuals or businesses

**Requirements for Video Editing:**

1. **Video Editing Software:** Proficiency in using video editing software such as Adobe Premiere Pro, Final Cut Pro, or DaVinci Resolve.
2. **Creativity:** Creative skills to enhance video content through effective editing techniques.
3. **Mindfulness:** Keen attention to detail to ensure seamless transitions, visual continuity, and audio synchronization.
4. **Technical Skills:** Understanding of video formats, codecs, and resolution for optimal output.
5. **Time Management:** Efficient time management to meet deadlines for video projects.
6. **Storytelling:** Ability to shape the narrative and flow of video content for maximum impact.

**Relevant Websites for Video Editing Resources:**

1. **Adobe Creative Cloud:** Provides access to Adobe Premiere Pro and other video editing tools.
2. **Final Cut Pro X:** Apple's professional video editing software for Mac users.
3. **DaVinci Resolve:** Offers advanced video editing and color correction capabilities.
4. **HitFilm Express:** A free video editing and visual effects software.
5. **YouTube Creator Studio:** Provides basic video editing tools for YouTube content creators.

Advantages of Video Editing:

1. **Visual Appeal:** Editing enhances the visual quality and aesthetics of videos.
2. **Storytelling:** Editing allows for effective storytelling through pacing and sequencing.
3. **Correction:** Mistakes and inconsistencies can be corrected during the editing process.
4. **Creative Freedom:** Video editing enables creative expression and experimentation.
5. **Professionalism:** Well-edited videos convey professionalism and engage viewers.

Disadvantages of Video Editing:

1. **Time-Consuming:** Editing can be time-consuming, especially for longer videos.
2. **Learning Curve:** Mastering video editing software requires time and practice.
3. **Technical Challenges:** Dealing with complex editing tasks may require technical expertise.
4. **Resource Intensive:** Video editing requires capable hardware for smooth performance.
5. **Subjectivity:** Creative choices might not always align with viewer preferences.

Video editing enhances video content, making it engaging and visually appealing. However, it involves a learning curve, potential technical challenges, and time commitment. Skilled video editors play a crucial role in shaping the final product and conveying messages effectively through visual storytelling.

# 23. AI Content Creation

### 23. AI Content Creation:

Use AI tools to generate content for blogs or websites.

**Requirements for AI Content Creation:**

1. **Understanding of AI Tools:** Familiarity with AI-powered content generation tools and platforms.
2. **Topic Knowledge:** Knowledge of the subject matter to guide AI in creating accurate content.
3. **Editing Skills:** Ability to review AI-generated content for quality and coherence.
4. **Creativity:** Skill in adding a human touch and creativity to AI-generated content.
5. **SEO Awareness:** Understanding of SEO principles to optimize AI-generated content for search engines.
6. **Adaptability:** Capacity to adapt to changes and improvements in AI content tools.

**Relevant Websites for AI Content Creation:**

1. **OpenAI's ChatGPT 3.5:** An AI language model for generating distinct types of content.
2. **ChatGPT Enterprise** A more sophisticated version of ChatGPT for business. It provides **GPT-4** access at high speeds and generates a diverse range of content.
3. **Articoolo:** Offers AI-powered article creation with a focus on unique content.
4. **Wordtune:** AI-powered platform for improving and enhancing written content.
5. **Writesonic:** Provides AI-generated content for marketing, blogs, and more.
6. **Copy.ai:** Offers AI-driven copywriting for various purposes.

**Advantages of AI Content Creation:**

1. **Time Efficiency:** AI-generated content reduces the time needed to produce articles, blogs, and more.
2. **Consistency:** AI ensures consistency in tone, style, and formatting.
3. **Variety of Content:** AI can generate content for different purposes and industries.
4. **Reduced Writer's Block:** AI can help overcome writer's block by generating starting points.
5. **Cost Savings:** AI-generated content can be cost-effective compared to hiring human writers.

**Disadvantages of AI Content Creation:**

1. **Quality Concerns:** AI-generated content might lack the nuanced understanding of human writers.
2. **Lack of Originality:** AI might generate content that is not entirely original or unique.
3. **Contextual Errors:** AI might misinterpret context, leading to inaccuracies.
4. **Human Touch:** AI-generated content can lack the human touch, empathy, and creativity.
5. **SEO Challenges:** AI-generated content may require additional optimization for search engines.

AI content creation offers efficiency and speed, but it comes with concerns about originality, quality, and contextual accuracy. Finding the right balance between AI-generated content and human creativity is key to leveraging the advantages while mitigating the disadvantages. Human oversight, editing, and value addition are crucial to producing high-quality and engaging content.

## 24. Online Research

### 24. Online Research:

Conduct research and compile reports for businesses or individuals.

## Requirements for Conducting Online Research:

1. **Information Literacy:** Strong ability to identify credible sources and reliable information online.
2. **Critical Thinking:** Skill in evaluating and analyzing online content for accuracy and relevance.
3. **Search Skills:** Proficiency in using search engines and online databases effectively.
4. **Data Collection:** Understanding of methods to gather and compile data from various sources.
5. **Organizational Skills:** Ability to organize and manage collected data and sources.
6. **Ethical Consideration:** Awareness of ethical guidelines in data collection and use.

## Relevant Websites for Online Research:

1. **Google Scholar:** Provides access to scholarly articles and research papers.
2. **PubMed:** Offers access to medical and life sciences research.
3. **JSTOR:** Digital library for academic journals, books, and primary sources.
4. **Wikipedia:** Provides a starting point for general information but you need to verify information from reliable sources.
5. **Statista:** Offers statistical data and reports across various industries.

**Advantages of Online Research:**

1. **Vast Resources:** Access to a wealth of information on a wide range of topics.
2. **Convenience:** Online research can be conducted from anywhere with an internet connection.
3. **Time Efficiency:** Online sources allow quick access to information, saving time.
4. **Diverse Perspectives:** Access to various viewpoints and sources enriches research.
5. **Cost Savings:** Online research reduces the need for physical materials and travel.

**Disadvantages of Online Research:**

1. **Credibility Issues:** Ensuring the credibility and reliability of online sources can be challenging.
2. **Information Overload:** Sorting through abundant information can be overwhelming.
3. **Limited Access:** Some valuable resources may be behind paywalls or subscription barriers.
4. **Outdated Information:** Online content might not always be up to date.
5. **Bias and Misinformation:** Online sources may contain biased or inaccurate information.

Online research provides a vast resource pool, but careful evaluation of sources is crucial to ensure credibility and reliability. The convenience and efficiency of online research are balanced by the need to navigate potential issues related to information quality, bias, and outdated content. Skillful research involves critical thinking and a discerning approach to using online sources effectively.

## Advantages of Side Gigs

1. **Additional Income:** They can provide extra money to supplement your primary income.
2. **Flexibility:** Side gigs can offer flexible working hours, giving you more choices about when and how much you work.
3. **Skill Development:** They can help you develop new skills or enhance existing ones.
4. **Pursue Passions:** They can often allow you to pursue your interests and passions outside of your regular job.
5. **Networking Opportunities:** Side gigs can provide opportunities to connect with new people and expand your professional network.

## Disadvantages of Side Gigs

1. **Time Commitment:** They require time and effort, which can be challenging to balance with your primary job and personal life.
2. **Financial Risks:** They may have upfront costs or inconsistent income, which can pose financial risks.
3. **Burnout:** Juggling multiple responsibilities can lead to burnout if not managed properly.
4. **Lack of Benefits:** Unlike full-time jobs, side gigs often do not offer benefits like healthcare or retirement plans.
5. **Competition:** Depending on the side gig, you may face competition from others offering similar services.

## Special Requirements

The requirements for each side gig will vary depending on the nature of the work. Side gigs may require specific skills, equipment, certifications, or licenses. It is important to research and understand the specific requirements for each one that you are interested in pursuing.

When considering a side gig, it is essential to assess your skills, interests, available time, and financial situation. Additionally, consider the market demand, competition, and potential risks associated with each side gig idea. This will help you make an informed decision and choose the right gig that aligns with your goals and circumstances.

## Disclaimer: Important Considerations

## Disclaimer: Important Considerations for Readers

While "24 Ways to Make Money Online with AI: Navigate Financial Challenges with Sustainable Side Gigs" provides valuable insights into capitalizing on AI opportunities, there are certain issues that the author cannot directly resolve for readers. It is essential to be aware of these aspects before embarking on your journey to financial success:

1. **Copyright and Intellectual Property:** The book may discuss AI-powered products and solutions, but it is crucial to understand that copyright and intellectual property regulations can vary across areas. You are advised to seek legal counsel or professional advice when developing, distributing, or profiting from AI creations to ensure compliance with copyright laws.

2. **Tax Implications:** Earning extra income through AI side gigs can have tax implications that differ based on your location and local tax regulations. The author cannot provide personalized tax advice. Talking to a certified tax professional or an accountant is a smart move. They can help walk you through the right actions to take when it comes to handling your taxes.

3. **Legal Compliance:** While this book suggests different ways to earn online, it is crucial to remember that online activities and making money are subject to rules and laws based on where you are located.

4. **Financial Risk:** While the book emphasizes the potential for financial stability and success, all investments, including time and effort spent on AI projects, carry inherent risks. You should carefully conduct your own due diligence before committing resources.

5. **Individual Circumstances:** How each strategy plays out can vary based on your own situation, skills, and the current market conditions. It is worth considering your unique circumstances and goals before delving into any of the strategies discussed in this book. '24 Ways to Make Money Online with AI' equips you with essential insights to embark on your journey toward financial growth. However, the author cannot address copyright issues, tax implications, legal compliance, or individual outcomes.

By being mindful of these considerations and seeking appropriate advice, you can navigate these complexities successfully and maximize the benefits of your AI-powered side gigs.

Wishing you success.

AAC

# Uncover the Secrets to Financial Success

In a world driven by technology, harnessing the power of artificial intelligence has never been more lucrative. This book unveils a compendium of 24 invaluable methods to capitalize on the AI revolution while engaging in flexible side gigs online.

**Thrive in the AI Boom.** With technology at your fingertips, you hold the key to unlocking diverse opportunities.

**Work on Your Terms** with a side gig that complements your lifestyle.

**Explore Limitless Industries** as you maximize your income streams and widen your horizons with AI's pervasive influence.

**Scale Your Success.** With automation at your disposal, you can take on more projects, elevate your earnings, and ascend the ladder of success.

**Future-Proof Your Journey.** AI isn't fleeting; it's a cornerstone of our future. By investing in online gigs and optimizing the use of AI, you ensure your relevance in an ever-evolving job market.

**Your financial future, empowered by AI, starts now.**